THE ART OF HERDING CATS

PART 1: LEARNING BY DOING LEADERSHIP

Monika Orski

THE ART OF HERDING CATS

Leading the Intelligent, A Mensa Experience

PART 1:

LEARNING BY DOING LEADERSHIP

© 2025 Monika Orski

Cover art by Natkacheva / Freepik

Published by BoD · Books on Demand, Östermalmstorg 1, 114 42 Stockholm, Sweden, bod@bod.se
Printed by Libri Plureos GmbH, Friedensallee 273, 22763 Hamburg, Germany

ISBN: 978-91-8080-982-5

Table of Contents

Introduction

Once upon a time, when I was young, I joined a funny little club called Mensa. I was a student of computer science and of literature – an unusual combination, I was often told. My confidence in being fairly intelligent was solid, but I had never done any kind of IQ test. Then I heard of this society that used high IQ as a requirement for entry, and that they would administer IQ tests. It wasn't even expensive to take one. Being a curious young woman, I decided to take their test, just for the fun of it. Then, I got an invitation to join Mensa. Still being curious, I decided to try a year of membership and see what it was all about.

Now, more than 30 years later, I know that this casual curiosity led me to a multi-fold adventure. Over the years, I have met many Mensans, had lots of fun, and travelled to places where I probably would not have gone to without a Mensa-related reason. Somewhere along the way, I learned a lot about interactions, different social and cultural contexts, and about leadership. More specifically, I learned how to lead Mensans, also known as herding cats. As you, being smart as you are, probably deduced from the title, these leadership lessons are the focus of this text.

Among many different volunteer positions, I was the chairperson (often simplified as "chair") of Mensa Sweden 2015-2019. During this time, I wrote a book called "Konsten att valla katter" ("The Art of Herding Cats"), that was published in 2019. It is a combination of a Mensa memoir and a leadership guide, or a hybrid between an essay and an instruction attempt. I am happy to have received plenty of positive reader response, as well as many interesting comments from readers; Mensans and non-mensans alike.

Since many of my Mensan friends do not read Swedish, and as no publishers has taken it upon them so far to translate the Swedish edition, I have tried to write on some of the same topics in English. This is not a translation. Partly because I could not translate from my native tongue into a foreign language. Partly because I now have the opportunity to try a new arrangement of the stories and add some ideas that have emerged in conversations after "Konsten att valla Katter" was published, as well as additional things I have learned in my continued volunteering in Mensa after the book was published in 2019. Consider this version as part of an ongoing adventure, one you are hereby invited to join.

This book consists of two parts, interwoven but still distinct:

The chapters marked as "*Memoirs of a Swedish Mensa dinosaur*" are memoirs of a sort. They tell the story of my experiences within Mensa Sweden, as I remember them. Needless to say, this is highly subjective, and other people involved in the same events might remember them differently. But it is my intention to let those parts show where my reasoning comes from, as well as to provide some entertainment.

The other chapters are intended as more practical leadership advice. If you are not interested in my more personal anecdotes, you are welcome to skip the memoirs chapters, as the advice and reflection parts can be read on their own.

Who Are Those Cats, anyway?

Leading members of Mensa, known as Mensans, is like herding cats. This has long been well established within the organization. We all are two-legged cats.

Cats are independent animals. If you annoy them, they will scratch you. They might scratch you when you have done nothing to annoy them, as well. Moreover, the two-legged cats are quick thinkers, and truly enjoy every opportunity to think. Their brains, restless and often easily bored, tend to look for the next shiny attraction. It's not an easy group to lead. On the other hand, no group is really easy to lead.

There are all sorts of cats. Mensa is known as the high-IQ society, because to become a member you have to take an IQ test and score within the upper 2% of the general population. This is the only thing all Mensans have in common. Apart from all being of proven high intelligence, Mensans are a very diverse group.

There is no other context where I find myself in such a diversified human environment. At a regular Mensa pub meeting in Stockholm, the age range around the table is from about 20 to over 70 of all conceivable professions. There are gardeners, engineers, physicians, taxi drivers, teachers, warehouse workers, musicians etc. Every time I think about it, a certain degree of fascination returns. Over the years, I have met hundreds of Mensans in dozens of different settings, and seen the very Mensan kind of conversations emerge in all those meetings.

It seems almost incredible that such a diverse group will find something to talk about. But somehow, the conversations around such a table, with all sorts of cats, always work out well. In fact, the conversation not only flows smoothly, but it also tends to cover anything and everything. A news item someone has read leads to discussions about space probes and possibilities of creating colonies on Mars. Someone starts talking about lab-grown meat, and within a few minutes, it leads to the question of whether the possibility of growing human meat would make our taboo against eating human flesh disappear. It's a context where you can rarely guess what will be discussed next, and where this unpredictability itself makes most people relax and have fun participating in the discussions.

Mensa is also a context where no one needs to prove anything. Even before coming to their first Mensa meeting, everyone who will be there has already demonstrated intelligence. It is firmly established from the start, and there is no need to reestablish this fact. Every time I hear someone speculate that Mensans would compete to show off their intelligence, I know that person has never been to a Mensa meeting. Of course, occasionally someone shows up who absolutely must assert themselves, as everywhere else. But they are few, and even those individuals usually understand that if they tried to do this by emphasizing their intelligence, they would make fools of themselves.

Curiosity Lured the Cat

Memoirs of a Swedish Mensa dinosaur, I

Curiosity made me a Mensan, although I had no idea at the time what that meant. I was curious to take an IQ test, and Mensa provided a simple way of having one. It was a sheer coincidence that I had learned something like Mensa even existed. A friend from secondary school who was studying in the US, told me he had heard of this strange High-IQ club. I didn't think much of it at the time, but I recognized the name when I saw a poster somewhere, inviting you to book an IQ test. The poster was probably at the Institute of Technology where I was a student, or maybe at the University where I studied literature at the same time. This was in 1991, and while I as a student of computer science had Internet access, there was as yet no notion of finding general information like this on the Internet.

Curiosity led me to the IQ test. I remember it was quite fun, but I thought it took ridiculously long to get a result. I had no idea that everything in Mensa Sweden was done on a strict volunteer basis, including scoring tests and mailing the results. Remember this was 1991, meaning everything was sent by snail mail. But finally, I got an answer, and an invitation to join Mensa Sweden. Curiosity did its trick again, and I decided to pay a year's dues to see what Mensa was about. I started receiving a member's magazine that looked like a fanzine, with different texts from different typewrites glued together on the pages. Here I learned that the Swedish section, or national Mensa as is the formal designation, was a small one – in fact, less than 300 members – but part of a larger international organization. I also learned that there were some in person Mensa meetings, and that most of the Swedish ones took place in my hometown Stockholm ...

It was only about a year later that curiosity roused me enough to attend one of those meetings. It was a small gathering, with quite a diverse group. Some were well into middle age. The youngest was still in secondary school. While I no longer remember what any of the discussions were about, I do remember that the atmosphere felt open and free, with ideas floating around and everyone taking part, talking in ways that I had not seen before in any group other than one of close friends. I tentatively decided to come back for more at some future meeting.

As the gathering was coming to an end, someone said that there should be a brief text about this meeting in the next magazine, and asked who can write it? No one seemed to eager to take on the task, although it was a small one. So at my first meeting, I volunteered. I wrote the short piece for the magazine.

The Volunteer Gene

Finding the right people for a job is always a challenge. Corporate recruitment is an art of its own, and one generally known to be difficult. When you need to find the right person to volunteer for a task or function, it gets even more difficult.

One of the most challenging and crucial aspects of an organization like Mensa is the constant need for volunteers. Moreover, it's essential to have the right type of volunteers for each task. This means that while it's a important to encourage interested individuals to step forward, it's not enough. Once they have, you also need to help them fit into the roles that need filling. Recruitment is essential.

However, the work is only half done when a volunteer has taken up the task. It's equally important to ensure that each volunteer receives follow-up and encouragement that matches their individual needs as close as possible. This includes encouraging people to advance within the organization, such as suggesting that someone who has volunteered in a role appointed by the board should now try to run for the board.

Hunting and Fishing – Finding Volunteers

You find candidates for a position through what one of my wise predecessors called "hunting and fishing." It's important to get to know many members so that you can ask those who seem suitable for a particular task. It's also important to advertise volunteer positions. This allows access to all members who want to express their interest, including new members who live somewhere where they are unlikely to meet any board members in the association's social settings. The first method is hunting; the second is fishing – a specific target versus a wide net.

In my experience, hunting is usually needed to fill the more difficult roles, while fishing is an excellent way to replenish already functioning committees while simultaneously making more people aware that volunteers are needed. Of course, fishing sometimes yields direct results for difficult roles too, but it is just as important that it indirectly makes future hunting easier.

When someone responds as a result of fishing, the person receiving the inquiry must respond quickly, and in several steps. The first step, of course, is to thank the member for wanting to spend their time volunteering. The next step is to ensure that the person understands what the task involves. As Mensa members generally grasp things quickly, it usually suffices to explain the purpose of the role and the approximate framework expected. If the person is still interested, then it's just a matter of trying it out. While you always need to know what to do if it doesn't work, be confident that it usually does.

Praise the Volunteers

Then, what makes these volunteers both want to and actually do the job? One of them, who has clearly found their niche and become part of Mensa Sweden's volunteer base, calls it the "volunteer gene." Maybe it truly is an innate tendency, an internal drive to get things done. Volunteer efforts are at best rewarded with gratitude and, hopefully, an occasional encouraging word from the board or other volunteers. However, the main reward for the time spent is nothing more than the joy of seeing what you have accomplished.

All this makes it even more important to show appreciation when you know how much time and effort people put into volunteer work. In any volunteer-based association, it is particularly important that the chairperson does. Knowing that I would not automatically praise often enough, I consciously tried to remember to do so whenever I saw the results of volunteer work.

Furthermore, a thank you on behalf of the association carries even more weight than one from the chairperson personally. In Mensa Sweden, we have established a routine of thanking our appointed volunteers with a letter and a small symbolic gift in December each year. The letters are printed on a regular computer printer, but the chairperson signs each one by hand. During my terms as chairperson, the gift consisted of two cinema tickets. The economic value is of course laughably small compared to the work being rewarded. But the essential message is that the effort is seen and appreciated. I often received appreciative comments about this annual symbolic gift. The trick may seem simple, but it is obviously effective.

Short- and Long-Term Planning

Praise and symbolic rewards apply once you have found volunteers, and they are doing what they are supposed to do. Most of the time, this works out well. Sometimes, it even turns out very, very well, with a new volunteer building on what already exists and managing to elevate an entire area to become significantly better than before. But then, you should not only applaud them. Instead, it's probably the right time to try to expand to have a group of helpers formed around this well-functioning area. We need to think ahead and look for new talents. The same principles apply here as in any other kind of organization: No one stays in a position forever. Nor should they.

For truly long-term planning, I usually suggest that you think about your successor's successor. The person who can take over a central function next should hopefully already be nearby. Otherwise, you must search quickly before it becomes urgent. Once things are as they should be, you can instead allow yourself to think about who can take over after that person. As chairperson I wanted especially to seek out those who might be good candidates for the chairperson position on the day when my successor steps back or is not re-elected. They must all be people inclined to volunteer, but it also pays to encourage them.

The Importance of an And

While the brand of two-legged cat called Mensan, i. e. the members of Mensa, is very diverse, most of us tend to have restless brains. You will find that when talking to a Mensan about what they do, in their professional life or as hobbies, you will typically hear a lot of "and". Someone is an IT-consultant who originally trained as a nurse. The next person is a carpenter, an architect, and a musician. Someone else is a professional dancer, singer and an engineer. Then you meet a physician who is also a professional creator of puzzles. Next, you happen to talk to someone who went from engineering to HR, and recently tried their hand at poetry. And so on.

While some highly gifted people do want to dig very deep into a specialty, most tend to explore multiple talent. Regarding talent, as in many things, the world is not fair; those who are really good at something, tend to also be good at other things. In an environment that expects you to be only one thing, whatever that would be, this can be frustrating. Therefore, one of the many social benefits of Mensa is the opportunity to meet a lot of people with one or several perfectly natural "and" in what they tell you they are doing.

Me? I'm a computer engineer, with the professional side quests of giving talks about leading intelligent people (also known as herding cats) and of publishing works of fiction as well as non-fiction. And I have done quite a bit of volunteer work in a wide range of areas, mostly for Mensa.

Stepping into Local Group and National Mensa
Memoirs of a Swedish Mensa dinosaur, II

Somehow, one instance of volunteering led to another, and then another. I went on to write other short articles for the magazine, Legatus Mensae. One of the ideas I had quite early, was to write recommendations rather than reviews, about books I liked and would recommend to others. It started with a casual, short piece now and then, but from late in 1995 I wrote one for almost every issue of the magazine. I still do.

It was easy to make casual friends in Mensa. While I had never before thought it particularly easy or interesting to hang out in groups, it felt different in this context. In Mensa, I found it a very welcoming environment as soon as I tried attending more meetings.

By then, I had learned that Mensa Sweden also had fairly independent local groups. There were still only a few of those, but the one in Stockholm was active and had at least a perfunctory part in organizing the in-person events I had come to like. Now, as I got more involved, I soon found myself part of the board of the local group. Not a great achievement in a small organization, but a nice way to feel involved, and a first lesson in being part of leadership.

Meanwhile, the then chairperson of Mensa Sweden was getting increasingly dissatisfied with his standing. In a board election in 1993, another candidate had challenged him. The incumbent won, but his reaction to being challenged was wanting more control of basically everything within Mensa Sweden. This reaction led to a backlash, which in turn led him to try and get rid of the people he thought were against his ideas of how to run an association. Various quarrels followed, and when the term was up in 1995 and it was time for another election, it was quite clear that this time, he would not be re-elected. His response was to disappear with the membership register and all other paperwork that had been in his care.

Mensa Sweden did survive this loss. There had been membership lists published to the members, which allowed at least a partial recreation of the register. As it was still a very small national Mensa, most of the active members knew each other, at least by name. But it did take time and effort to get the association working again. At this point, I already thought Mensa important enough to be worth an effort, and of course, I volunteered. I did my small part of the work needed to get it all up and running again.

I stayed on the board of the Stockholm local group, now better synchronized with the national Mensa. At some point, when the local group needed a new chair, I let myself be persuaded into volunteering again. So, there I was, hosting board meetings in my studio. I would make some simple sandwiches for the meeting and open a bottle of wine; we had our discussions and somehow seemed to get things done.

This was also the time when I really saw the benefits of being part of an international association, with the experiences and contacts provided by such an organization. In 1996, Mensa celebrated its 50-year anniversary, by a large gathering in London. Going there, I found that even in the context of hundreds of Mensans, the ease of contact felt quite like it did at small gatherings of 5-6 people, only on a much larger scale. It was a fun event to attend, and as far as I remember, this was also the first time that I heard the saying that "leading Mensans is like herding cats".

While Mensa was still not particularly well known in Sweden, we were starting to get some more attention, and more members. One important factor was an early Internet presence. A simple web page created by a member attracted interest, as society was digitizing. Then, some media coverage helped, although most of the articles were mostly about discovering the existence of this strange IQ club.

I remember a young man talking to me in a bar. He probably wasn't particularly interested in striking up conversation with me, but his friend was trying to chat up my friend. I have no idea why he felt the need to assert himself, but he claimed to be a member of Mensa, obviously aiming to impress. I replied that then he would know the name of the chairperson of the local group, to which I got a blank look.

"That would be me", I said, holding out my hand to shake. "Nice to meet you."

This proved an even more effective way to scare him off then telling people in bars that I was a computer engineer.

Somehow, as the years went by, Mensa Sweden was growing quite fast. From a dip to around 200 members in 1995, it was nearing 600 around 2000. Around that time, I was asked whether I would like to join the national board. And I volunteered. In 2001, I ran for the office of vice chair, and I was elected.

Leadership Means Responsibility

Among the most common clichés I hear about leadership is the phrase "take responsibility." Among the most common mistakes I've seen from individuals in some form of leadership position is the inability to understand and prove equal to everything that actual responsibility entails.

Yet this is fundamentally simple, at least at the level of general principles. The responsibility creed of a functioning leader is: When things go wrong, it's my fault.

This attitude needs to be maintained outwardly under all circumstances. Never blame anyone else in public. Never, not even when you had no idea what was going on. This may feel difficult to implement, but in truth it's not only among a leader's duties – it also pays off. In my experience, this approach leads to being respected, even by most of the people who disagree with you. The opposite tactic, to start a blame game and look for scapegoats, invariably leads to a lack of respect for the person presumed to function as chairperson, manager, director, or indeed leader of any kind.

My Fault and Their Merit

When a nonprofit organization's board works well, it's the merit of the entire board. When it doesn't, it's the chairperson's fault. Of course, it can be more or less difficult to make it work, depending on the individuals on the board. As chair of Mensa Sweden, I was fortunate, blessed with mostly very good boards. It might seem easy to say that it would be my fault if it didn't work when, in fact, it did work. But I am convinced that even with a board consisting of excellent people, this attitude is one of the key factors for success. I have seen many cases where it hasn't worked out despite decent conditions, precisely because they had a chair who refused to see their responsibility to make it work.

However, the chair's responsibility does not end with ensuring the board's work flows smoothly. It applies to everything that happens in the organization's name, both within it and in external contacts. To step in and take care of something that has gone wrong where you weren't even involved can be highly challenging, but that's part of the leadership deal. If you're not willing to get in the way of the mess when things go wrong, you're not the right person for the job.

Praise Publicly, Criticize Privately

The ultimate responsibility lying with the chairman does not, of course, prevent the need to acknowledge those who have done a good or bad job on a particular matter. It is also part of the chair's duties to ensure that people know what has gone well or poorly.

Praise can be given publicly. Mention it at a board meeting or even at a large organization gathering. Send a plaque, shout it from the rooftops... Simply ensure that as many people as possible know that someone has done something particularly well. But stay aware of a small caveat here: Some individuals absolutely do not want to receive public praise. You need to gauge what each person specifically prefers, case by case. If you cannot gauge it, just ask them. There is absolutely no reason to force public applause on someone who is uncomfortable with it.

On the other hand, criticism should be conveyed privately, solely to the person concerned. Sometimes, the rest of the board may need to know that you have had such a conversation with an officer or appointed volunteer. However, other than a statement of the fact that you had a talk, nothing should be heard beyond the room where you express what you have to say, solely to the person it concerns.

Leadership by Sugar

The best and most general leadership trick I know is so simple, I am a little ashamed to admit that it's the single trick that works best. My best trick is, in fact, to put a bowl of sweets on the table, or assorted chocolate pralines, or a few mixed bags of candy in general. I call it "leadership through sugar." It works with cats, and with basically everyone else.

The Blood Sugar Factor

Take a moment to consider the effect of low blood sugar on an average work meeting. People who normally get along perfectly well start snapping at each other. Minor differences of opinion that usually create an interesting discussion toward consensus turn into people not talking to each other or, in the worst case, only talking to say that the other is a complete idiot. But if you take a break, ask everyone to get coffee or tea or whatever they want to drink and put out a bowl of candy, it can work miracles. Ideally, of course, you should do this before colleagues have started yelling at each other.

This is, of course, as applicable in a Mensa board meeting as it is in the workplace. Therefore, I made sure to have plenty of sugar on the table for the board meetings I chaired. What used to be sandwiches when the local chapter's board met at my home evolved into candy on the table at the national board's meetings in rented premises. Of course, we would also go out for lunch before getting too tired. Still, the principle is the same.

In fact, this worked out so well, we didn't have any direct quarrels within the boards I led. There were occasions when we didn't agree and had to vote on the matter, but we did not quarrel. Occasionally disagreeing is healthy. If everyone always agreed, there would be no reason to talk about things and weigh different arguments. What matters is keeping the discussion at the right level, and preferably on a factual level that allows for results acceptable for everyone, whether through compromise or by voting. I'll leave it unsaid how much sugar has affected that, but I am convinced it has played a role.

For that matter, the same trick works excellently for gatherings that are less formal than board work. When I have led groups of volunteers to organize various activities within the association, I have also used leadership through sugar. Inviting the group for planning and offering them a glass of wine or soda with simple snacks has been a winning concept with all sorts of volunteer groups and committees.

Equally Applicable in Paid Work

Moreover, sugar is indeed highly applicable in the workplace as well. The first time I used it in a professional environment was when I had to act as a supervisor for a larger group. It was an incredibly instructive but very confusing project that made me realize that project management was definitely not the path I wanted to continue professionally; but that's another story. The project required a lot of overtime and was stressful for many in the group I was assigned to lead. The fact that the group was highly diverse in both knowledge and ambition levels didn't make it any easier. We all worked in a large office, with multiple workstations at each table. It was quite crowded, but in the middle of the room, there was some free table space. After a few weeks, I made it a habit to put candy there, along with a pack of pain relief pills for those with literal headaches. I won't claim that leadership went smoothly after that, but it certainly became much easier.

Sure, it's simple. But think again about what fatigue and low blood sugar can do to perfectly reasonable people, not to mention what a sense of someone seeing and trying to improve the situation can do to get people in a better mood. Sometimes, the simplest tricks are also the best.

Feed the Restless Brain

In volunteer work as well as in business, it is an important challenge to keep the good people you managed to find, be they employees or volunteers. Regarding employment, money, vacation time, and other benefits are always important factors. To quote a saying from the IT-business: "If you pay peanuts, you get monkeys." But while a fair salary and the related benefits are necessary, they are usually not enough to keep your intelligent employees. Because just like in their volunteer work, they need to feed their restless brains.

Everyone needs variation. But Mensans tend to need more variation than most people. The highly intelligent brain needs to be fed, and one good way of feeding it is to explore new things. Knowing this leads to an important insight when working with the highly intelligent, whether it is paid work or volunteer work. The default should not be trying to find someone who has already done whatever you are recruiting for. What you really want is to find someone who has the basic skills necessary to quickly learn what you will want them to do.

Then, when your two-legged cat has learned new skills and used them for a while, they should be offered the opportunity to learn something new again. This is how you keep cats interested: once a certain task is done, let them chase the next, shiny challenge.

To Handle Growth and Steal Duels
Memoirs of a Swedish Mensa dinosaur, III

When I became the vice chair of Mensa Sweden in 2001, our little club had already grown well beyond being just a little club. It has kept growing since, now being the national Mensa with the largest per capita membership, around 8000 members while Sweden has around 10 million inhabitants. Part of this growth was probably caused by media coverage, part by an early Internet presence, and part by the fact that belonging to associations of different kinds is very common in Sweden. This is also the case in our neighbouring countries, who also have high per capita memberships. But when Mensans around the world ask how we managed to get such high numbers, the answer is that we do not really know what we are doing right, we can only try not to stop doing it.

While growth was nice, especially as it brought active Mensa groups to smaller cities where there had previously only been a few members, growth also took its toll on the organization. With nearly 1000 members, it was no longer feasible to have volunteers do the entire administration. The workload was simply too much. The board I served on worked to find ways of using paid help for certain tasks. While that did work out fine after a while, it took a while to make things functioning and stable. At national level, I learned that there is always another problem to handle, somewhere. But being part of a national board was a rewarding experience. Working with a very good chair was also a rewarding experience, even more so as his management style was very different from mine. I learned a lot. Among many practical things, he taught me that there is usually more than one way of doing things right and getting them done.

Another task that came with this board, was to update the statutes of Mensa Sweden, called Bylaws. With a growing and now nationwide organization, it was high time to update the Bylaws. This was quite a lot of work, most of which was done by the chair and the board secretary. But everyone on the board got involved to some extent, and I can boast of having one particular impact. I suggested that the water pistol duel should be written into the Bylaws, as it was and still is.

Now, I cannot claim to have come up with the original idea. I proudly stole if from Mensa Hungary. It had been mentioned on an international Mensa mailing list that I was part of. Having a water pistol duel as one way of solving (not very grave) conflicts within the society has proved a very popular rule, even though it isn't used very often.

From the Bylaws of Mensa Sweden:

Settlement by Duel

If all parties involved in a dispute agree to resolve the dispute by duel, a water pistol duel is to be held. After the duel, the dispute is to be considered settled, and no further sanctions will be imposed.

Regulations of the water pistol duel are to be specified by the board in a separate document. No member can be forced to resolve a dispute by duel or sanctioned for not agreeing to duel.

By then the growing association had established the habit of a social annual gathering for all its members, rotating between different cities each year. As the number of members was growing, so was the number of participants to these gatherings. For the one in 2004, a member in Stockholm had taken it upon himself to coordinate the organization. But as the time of the gathering drew near, it became clear that while he would help with some of the work, he would not be able to coordinate it. The location was to be Stockholm, and I was the only board member living in Stockholm ... This time I didn't really have the choice not to volunteer.

While the gathering was a small one compared to what we have today – around 95 participants compared to around 700 – it was quite a lot of work. But once it was on, participants seemed happy, and meeting a bunch of Mensans was as fun as always, although there was a bit of stress in trying to herd all those cats together. I did demand satisfaction from the original coordinator, challenging him to a duel on the last day of the gathering weekend. As we duelled in the rain, it was difficult to determine who won, but I claim that I did, and he accepted this with good grace. It did work; after duelling there were no hard feeling between us.

During my time as vice chair, I also had the opportunity to experience the IBD table. IBD, the International Board of Directors, is the governing body of Mensa International, mostly composed of the chair from each national Mensa. It meets once a year, a meeting of dozens of people from different cultures trying to get things done together. As the Swedish chair couldn't attend the 2002 meeting, he sent me as his proxy. Quite an experience, with the very special impact of such a diverse round table.

After being re-elected vice chair once, I stepped down in 2005. I had decided that it was time for me to go back to being an ordinary Mensa member for a while. I would still write my book recommendations for the magazine, and organize some local meetings, including the start of a Mensan book club that is still active.

The Difficult Art of Delegation

As a leader, it's easy to end up with far too much to do. I strongly suspect that this pattern is particularly strong in all associations where things get done by volunteer work, regardless of the association's purpose. Everything that hasn't been done tends to end up at the table of the chair, and the chair becomes everyone's ultimate backup in times of trouble. Questions and problems usually find their way to the leader. Unless you are careful, the workload will become impossible.

What to do to reduce the workload? Delegate! people often exclaim. Which, indeed, is not bad advice but also not very helpful if not elaborated. Delegation is far from being as easy as it sounds.

What to delegate?

First and foremost, it's important to know what to delegate. In order to understand what to delegate, you must be able to break down tasks into manageable parts. But this can be difficult, because things tend to be interconnected. Therefore, creating manageable parts is all about finding chunks that somehow can be managed on their own. A certain amount of time will also be needed for overlap, discussions, and information transfer. The secret, of course, is to ensure that this necessary overhead time is significantly less than the time it takes to do everything yourself.

Delegating tasks is primarily about obtaining long-term relief. Therefore, you need to shift your focus from the time and effort required for a handover and instead consider the time saved when essentially the same thing needs to be done for the fifth time. A proper handover, in turn, requires a lot of preparatory work, including clear delimitation of the responsibilities of the person you intend delegating to. It is, in my experience, extremely rare that mind-reading works. What is not said aloud, and preferably repeated, will not be understood and kept in mind.

Always to one person

Then, of course, it's important to delegate tasks to the right person. The right person is someone who wants to do it and can do it, i.e. a person who not only is able to handle the task but also is genuinely willing to perform it. It can be quite difficult to determine if someone is willing or just claims to be, as the latter usually isn't a deliberate lie but merely the result of an overly optimistic view of how many hours can be fit into a day.

You learn from your mistakes, and from the mistakes other people make. Having seen a person take on tasks that remains undone, I will know that this person is not a good candidate for delegating new tasks. The association's reliable workhorses who have already completed many other tasks in the past, however, might end up with more work if they don't duck. The old saying that in order to get something done, you should as someone already busy, usually holds true.

Another general rule is always to delegate tasks to a person, not a group. Of course, it's perfectly fine to have a group or committee working together but always make sure there is someone responsible for the group's work being carried out. Without such a leader who has a clearly stated responsibility, it simply won't get done.

The Command at the End of the Road

Some things are different when leading volunteers compared to any kind of formal leadership in a workplace. There are differences in mutual expectations, and in time frames. And then, there is the difference regarding the option of an end of the road command.

Discussions are usually a good thing. They lead to better understanding and can spur better ideas. Being from a very consensus centred culture myself, I know that in an international environment I sometimes even leave too much time for discussion. But while it is important to let everyone in the group be heard, consensus will not always result. In some cases, within an association, you vote; and the majority decision stands. Other cases will mirror professional life, where someone is in charge and has the right to make the decision.

In a professional setting, there is always the possibility of a definitive command. If I am your boss, I could say "now you do this the way I tell you to, because that is what you are paid for". I can honestly say that, in a long career including different leadership roles, I have never said anything like it. If I ever do, I will consider it the kind of professional failure that would make me question whether I should take on jobs including leadership ever again. But the point here is that when I am your boss, you know and I know that I could say this, and that command would be a definitive end of discussion.

Now, working with volunteers adds an extra challenge. I can hardly tell them "now you do this the way I tell you to, because that is ... what you are not paid for ..." It is not only desirable but necessary that they want to do the work. And this, in turn, is a reason why leading volunteers is excellent leadership training.

The Mysteries of Pedagogical Explanation

In every job, as with any voluntary assignment, an essential starting point is understanding what you are expected to do. Therefore, anyone who is, in some way, tasked with leading the work of others must also be able to explain both what needs to be done and, to a reasonable extent, how it should be done. The principles for doing this sensibly are the same regardless of the audience, but if you know that the recipient is highly intelligent, it may be beneficial to adjust certain details by changing the order in which you present things.

The Famous Stonecutters

Many readers are likely to be familiar with the instructive story of the two stonecutters. There are a few variations, but the essence is as follows:

A man arrives at a quarry where several stonecutters are hard at work. He approaches one and asks what she is doing.

"I am shaping this block of stone to be rectangular with sufficiently smooth sides", she replies.

The man moves on, stops at another stonecutter and poses the same question. This stonecutter's response is different.

"I take part in building a cathedral!"

The conventional moral of the story is that the second stonecutter's response is better. People should see the bigger picture and understand the purpose of their work. I am not going to dispute this; it is important to be aware of what the work ultimately aims to achieve. However, it is also important to remember that if the stonecutter is only told she is building a cathedral, she will have no idea what she actually needs to do. Before any work can be meaningfully carried out, she must find out what sort of cathedral the architect and builder have in mind and how far construction has progressed, then collaborate with every other stonecutter involved, to allocate the next layer of stone blocks among themselves.

To ensure that people understand what needs to be done, it is necessary to provide them with the overall objective that the organisation aims to achieve, but also a practical level of definition for their individual tasks. The stonecutter needs to know that her task for the immediate future is to deliver a specific number of blocks of specific dimensions for the foundation of one of the cathedral's towers. However, every thoughtful worker should have the autonomy to decide how best to complete their task. Avoid trying to tell the stonecutter which tools to use.

The Goal and the Path

There is a common mistake that many people make when teaching someone a new task. They start by explaining the first step, then the second, then the third – and around that point, it is often time to take a break and perhaps resume with the next step the following day.

Why is this wrong? Because the initial step of any explanation should be indicating the destination. Begin by pointing out the house in the distance that the road leads to. Then, it is time to take that first step, followed by the second, and so on.

An example from my computerized daily work to illustrate this: if you are introducing someone to a new development environment, you should start by explaining what it is intended for, such as being an environment for Java development with links to a version-controlled code base for various projects. Next, move on to the first step: installing the environment. Then comes logging in and configuration. After that, you can show where the relevant projects for the programmer's current work can be found. And so on from there.

Special Considerations for the Gifted

The above principles apply to all explanations, regardless of who the recipient is. However, if you know that the person receiving the explanation is highly intelligent, there are a couple of adjustments to further enhance the process.

The first piece of advice may seem trivial; You can move faster. Not only is it possible to spend less time than usual explaining each step, but it is actually advantageous to do so, as this reduces the risk of the listener becoming distracted. Consider skipping a few intermediate steps in the explanation of each section. Highly intelligent recipients are likely to not only be capable of filling in these gaps themselves, but also to appreciate the opportunity to do so.

The second point is less obvious but surprisingly effective with many of those gifted. This involves taking things somewhat out of the usual order. Start as normal by pointing out the house that the path leads to but also provide a few more details about the destination before circling back to the first step. Mention that when you arrive, you will need to reach the fourth floor, and it might be a bit challenging as there is no lift. Let your audience be aware of this challenge while you proceed to explain the path, albeit at a faster pace than usual.

The Ombudsman's Remit
Memoirs of a Swedish Mensa dinosaur, IV

For about three years, I managed to stay out of elected volunteer positions. Then, in 2008, there was a need for a new ombudsman within Mensa Sweden. The then chair, a friend and highly respected Mensan, asked me to run. It was a bit of hunting, although this was an elected position and not one appointed by the board. Prompted like this, I did what I do – I volunteered. As there was no other candidate at this point, I was automatically elected.

An ombudsman in Mensa is primarily charged with arbitrating disputes within the association, mostly regarding conflicts between individual members and the rights of the organisation as such. But the specific remit of the ombudsman position within Mensa Sweden also includes being the volunteer charged with ensuring that other volunteers do not violate the association's internal rules. This part of the remit is sometimes referred to as the ombudsman also being a non-fiscal auditor, or an examining body with respect to other offices.

While the disputes part occasionally involved gathering facts that led to recommending the board taking some sort of disciplinary action, the bulk of complaints that reached the ombudsman proved to be quite easily handled. The typical issue would be concerning a member seriously misbehaving at a meeting. I would call the member on the phone, introduce myself and say that I heard something happened at this meeting, and that before saying anything I wanted to hear their side of the story. In an overwhelming majority of the cases, the member's first line would be

"I have done nothing wrong!"

And then, after a few minutes of mostly that person retelling me the story in their own words, they would say

"Yes, that was a rather bad thing to do. I don't know what I was thinking. It won't happen again."

The second part of the ombudsman's remit, to ensure that the board follows the Constitution and Bylaws, did not take much work in my first ombudsman term. As I went on to a second three-year term, things gradually evolved to make this a more difficult task. First, there were some minor irregularities to note. Then, with a new chair, the problems grew. The chair put himself in a situation where he had to step down, and an inexperienced vice chair had to become chairman. While no one on the board had the intention to hurt the association or anyone in it, they were not able to properly lead, and the new chair was unable to keep up to his responsibilities. The general meeting where it was my duty as ombudsman to report this was quite an intense one. However, this inexperienced chair showed his good intentions by also stepping down, in an orderly manner.

I was still relieved that this general meeting also marked the end of my term as ombudsman. The ombudsman function would be in good hands, as the only candidate for the position was the former chair whose vice chair I had been ten years earlier. And I happily intended to go back to being a regular member for at least a few years. That didn't last, though.

Complaints

Something you learn in an association, regardless of the type of association, is that among the people attracted to it, there is a category who really enjoys association settings: people with constant complaints. Do not deceive yourself into thinking that you can change this phenomenon. You must be able to handle it.

The Perpetually Dissatisfied

The individuals who always come up with one complaint after another should not be confused with those who occasionally have perfectly valid objections to the way something is being handled or not handled. The latter category is a great asset, as they make you aware of things that do not work. Usually, they are also prepared to help improve what they have complained about.

The perpetually dissatisfied are something entirely different. Fortunately, they are few, but they tend to be loud. These people are characterized by:

• They know everything without needing to look into any facts or gain any understanding of the context.

• Their way of doing things is not only better; it is the only right way.

• They are very upset that those who spend their free time running the association have the audacity to have their own opinions on how this should be done.

Does anyone think this category diminishes in an association where the only common factor among all members is a high IQ? I must disappoint you. It seems to be just as common in Mensa as in any other association.

Instead, since these people are also used to feeling smart, they often become extremely irritated if their opinions are met with actual arguments, not to mention how insulted they are if told to read a text of perhaps 2-3 pages to understand the background. The big problem with this category of members is that although they make up a very small proportion of the membership, they can easily steal an incredible amount of time and energy from the volunteers who are in fact getting things done.

This is essentially the same phenomenon as the typical internet troll; people who find pleasure in making things difficult for others. There are examples in Mensa's international history where the perpetually complaining have even managed to take over national boards. Since their only real interest is complaining, this has always resulted in them switching to complaining about each other until their society practically disintegrated and had to be rebuilt. Rebuilt by others, of course.

Handling Complaints

While an association falling apart is an extreme and rare consequence, you need to be aware of the complaints problem and have a clear strategy to handle it. In my view, the strategy starts with the point that it's the chair's problem and should therefore not steal time from anyone else. In general, all problems that land with the board are the chair's problems, and all other board members should be able to pass them on to their chair and trust that the problems will be handled there. Sometimes they will be handled well, sometimes not particularly well, but it is the chair's responsibility to get it done.

It has certainly happened more than once in my years as chair that I grumbled about something at the pub after a board meeting, but it was still me and no one else who should take care of the problem. This is the first and most important step to prevent the perpetually complaining from causing too much trouble.

The second step is to have a strategy for the practical side of receiving this kind of complaints. Mine was basically to try and act like a duck, with the perpetual complaints being water. Just let it roll off, wash past in a general noise of ideas and impressions. Complaints simply go along with everything else down the duck feathers. The key is not to take it personally. It is not me they are complaining about; it is their abstract image of a chair, and that usually not only lacks connection with my person but also with the actual role itself.

Then there is a fantastic trick. When someone complains that something is not done the way they want, the perfect response is, "so you want to do it yourself?" In nine out of ten cases, you will not hear from that person again ... at least not until a week later, when they have found the next thing to complain about.

Zero Jerk Tolerance

Ongoing complaints from a few perpetually dissatisfied people have to be tolerated, at least to a certain extent. However, no one should have to endure being treated badly by people they are supposed to work with. This applies to volunteers just as it obviously should apply to any workplace.

The author Robert Sutton uses the term "The No Asshole Rule" as a book title, and I have proudly stolen that term for use in both Mensa and work life. Sutton's book, which I recommend, is about building civilized workplaces by not tolerating bullying behaviour. The principle can be applied to any environment that should be civilized.

Everyone can occasionally say something that they, upon reflection, should not have said. I am certainly aware that this happens to me. The real dividing line is what happens next. Does the person back down, perhaps even apologize, and try to avoid repeating their bad behaviour? Or does the person loudly insist on how right they are and how everyone else is stupid? I have seen adults behave roughly like three-year-olds who do not get their way and have no illusions about always being able to reason with people. This applies to highly gifted, intelligent people about as often as everyone else.

Therefore, it is important to uphold the principle that no one, regardless of their contributions otherwise, has the right to harm others. Sure, you can see it as a matter of morality and civilization, but you can also be very practical and transactional about it. There is absolutely no one so valuable that the association or company does not lose greatly by letting that person scare others away from the group by behaving badly towards them. In short, you must make clear that jerks are not welcome.

Chair at the Table
Memoirs of a Swedish Mensa dinosaur, V

After I had ended my second ombudsman term, I was not entirely out of volunteer work for Mensa. The chair, who was in charge of getting the organization fully functional again after a year of relative chaos, did entice me to help the board with some IT-related investigations, meaning I was still a bit involved. Even so, I could consider myself a free Mensan, not in office.

However, towards the end of that year, the chair had decided not to run for the next full term as chair. The year of cleaning work had taken its toll. No other, good candidates seemed quite willing, either. In the meantime, I had been thinking that I might want to run for chair at some future point. Now, seeing this situation, I needed to make a quick decision on whether the time would be sooner rather than later. I talked to people close to me and thought hard about it for a few days. Then, I volunteered.

When elected chairperson in 2015, I had recently been warned by the then ombudsman that he would need to put a difficult task to the board. I had, in fact, narrowly escaped having to deal with it as ombudsman myself, as the situation had escalated to formal handling only a few days after he took over. The situation? A long-time member, a man well into middle age, who over the years, had gone from trying to be more intimate than most would appreciate, to downright harassing several female members. He would no longer respect a "no", and there were multiple reports of him frightening other members to the extent that they no longer wanted to attend Mensa meetings. Before this formally became a matter for the ombudsman, other members had tried to talk to him. Now, the ombudsman had put in months of effort to make him understand what he was doing and stop the harassment, but to no avail. It was now a matter of disciplinary action, and to expel a member from Mensa Sweden (as the rules were at the time), the board would have to put a motion to the General Meeting.

While that expulsion case certainly loomed over the board, there were also many other things that needed attention. I was lucky to have a good board, where everyone was ready to get the work done. Despite hard work from the board of the previous "clean up" year, some parts were still not quite up and running again. We set out to get them done, for example to find volunteers to maintain and modernize the organization's IT. There was of course also the everyday workload of a board, things big and small. I started tracking the time I put into Mensa board work as chair and found that on average it summed up to 10-15 hours per week.

The board found its rhythm and ways of working. 2015 turned to 2016. And despite continuous efforts to find a solution to the disciplinary matter without making it an expulsion case, no such solution had been found. When it was time for the 2016 General Meeting, the board had agreed that unfortunately, the only way to rectify the situation with the member who kept harassing other members was to move that the General Meeting would expel him. Neither of us wanted to do this, but an unanimous board decided we had to. What was right was right. As a chair, I knew it was part of the job I had taken upon me to be the face of our decision. As could be expected, there was quite an explosion of questions, and of strange suspicions aired about the board as well as the victims of harassment. My primary duty as chair was to shield those victims as well as the other board members as best I could, but then also to speak on behalf of the board at the actual meeting. The discussion went on for hours. In the end, a very clear majority, almost 90%, of the votes cast were in favour of the expulsion. A much better outcome than the alternative, but I still found it difficult to smile when well-meaning Mensans congratulated me on the result.

We were all exhausted after that General Meeting. As for me, I was not only tired in general, but very tired of being the target of all sorts of strange conspiracy theories spread by people who didn't want to acknowledge the result of a General Meeting vote. In the following weeks, I felt that I was just about able to muster enough strength to keep up chair work for the two-year term I had committed to. But then the usual, general work went on. I went to some social Mensa meetings, including a large European one, and found some kind of working rhythm again.

Another ongoing task was one I had promised to take on when running for office: to try and find a way to provide easily accessible IQ tests (Mensa entry tests) for teenagers under 18, i. e. still underage. It took some systematic search to find a psychologist willing to volunteer to investigate what this would entail under Swedish law. Then, her investigation needed time, of course. Finally, she reported that it would be possible under certain circumstances, but she didn't want to take on the task of providing those tests herself. I needed to find another child psychologist who would. It did work out, eventually, but only towards the end of my first two-year term as chair. It took patience. I was still very happy that I managed to deliver on my promise. Things take time.

As chair, I got more involved in the international aspects of Mensa. I was now the Swedish representative to IBD, the International Board of Directors. I was also part of the regional network of Nordic Chairs, the chairs of Mensa Denmark, Finland, Norway and Sweden. This small network of peers would be an essential part of keeping my mental health during sometimes difficult leadership times. To have peers to share with is a great source of support. But the Nordic chairs network also resulted in several ideas about common projects. The most important of those would be the Nordic Mensa Fund, a regional foundation to support intelligence research. The idea was conceived during a chairs meeting in Stockholm in 2016, and the Fund was formally created in 2020, following decisions by the four Annual General Meetings in 2019. Things take time.

When my first term as chair was nearing its end in 2017, I decided to run for another term. I felt that I wasn't quite finished yet. And apparently the membership agreed. As no other candidate stepped forward, I was automatically re-elected for another two-year term.

People with High Standards

Highly gifted individuals often set high standards for themselves. This can be an incredible asset, but it can also be a weakness. Some establish ambitious goals and work diligently, albeit sometimes inconsistently, to achieve these targets. Coupled with the typical restless brain of an intelligent person, it can occasionally appear as if these individuals cannot make up their minds. It often reflects their capacity to manage and accomplish a multitude of tasks. This is energy worth harnessing; for themselves, for employers lucky enough to hire such people, and for organisations fortunate enough to engage them as volunteers.

Some of these individuals may tire after a while. They need variety and are drawn to new places where they can showcase their abilities. This is not necessarily a reflection on the employer or the organisation. Many highly intelligent people simply have a low threshold for losing interest. Within Mensa, we naturally want these gifted individuals to stay and remain active, making it essential to offer a wide range of volunteer opportunities and new roles to explore.

High standards can also be a disadvantage at times. Constantly demanding peak performance from oneself makes it difficult to live up to your own expectations, and this can severely impair self-confidence. Highly gifted individuals sometimes need to be reassured that they are not expected to perform at their absolute best all the time. It is enough to bring out that top capacity when it is genuinely needed and, at other times, to maintain a steady level that is sustainable over the long term. Often, this "steady" level is already above average – a fact that many high-performing intelligent people struggle to recognize.

But then, those with very high expectations of themselves tend to impose similar expectations on others. This is generally a poor approach. Others will never consistently meet such high demands. This holds true not just in the workplace but also in environments where everyone is an intelligent volunteer. A key lesson is that a Mensa member who demands constant peak performance from everyone is destined to be a poor leader. I have witnessed national chairs of various associations render themselves deeply unpopular, and sometimes even cause their respective Mensa chapters to shrink, because of this mistake.

Authority is Earned, not Given

It is sometimes said that in the corporate world, intelligent employees often have some difficulty concerning authority. Perhaps there is indeed some statistical correlation there. In that case, I am not aware of it. However, it is very clear that for people who can and want to think for themselves, authority is something that must be earned. Having a title or a formal position is not enough.

Who has authority?

An acquaintance from Mensa shared a story that, for me, encapsulates the difference between distrusting authority and simply not recognizing authority where it hasn't been earned. He was being treated by a psychologist and had simultaneous contact with a caseworker from the relevant authority. When the psychologist mentioned that he seemed to have difficulty with authority figures, the Mensa member initially didn't understand what the psychologist was talking about.

"Yes, like how you talk about this caseworker you interact with ... "

"That little wimp is no authority!"

No, evidently, that caseworker was no authority for this Mensa member. Whether it was justified or not, I have no idea.

A Matter of Trust

The question how to earn authority falls into the category of questions truly impossible to answer. It is clearly impossible to establish simple guidelines. However, I believe in implementing the mindset that authority is something that should be earned, not something you already have or, worse, expect to be given. You must also remember that it takes time to establish an authoritative position because fundamentally, it's a matter of trust. Trust can be destroyed quickly, but it always takes a long time to build.

A general piece of advice is to dare to be direct. State what is expected and what is and is not acceptable. Those who can set clear and reasonable boundaries show that they are ready to take on the role, ready to lead when needed. This of course also includes the courage to make mistakes and admit when you were wrong. People who believe they are perfect won't get far in gaining the trust necessary to, ultimately, be regarded as an authority. Also keep in mind that highly intelligent people are generally both creative and adept at understanding others, so if you bluff, there's a good chance they will know.

The Infamous Extra Mile

Another key to authority is always demanding a little more from yourself than from anyone else. You might not literally walk that mythical extra mile, but you will need to put in some more work than you ask of anyone else. While expecting extra effort from others has become quite infamous in many industries, setting healthy but high expectations of your own effort remains a sign of leadership by example.

A board who sees the chair putting in a bit more effort than expected from them, will consider that chair a person worth listening too – at least if the effort is used for some reasonable purpose. Other volunteers will give the same respect, not only for the chair but also when asked to do things by board members who are willing to invest a bit more time and effort then they ask from others.

Opinions Can Change

Sometimes, your opinion or your idea of how things should be done changes with time. You get new information, you see how something you tried turns out, or your priorities shift. Sometimes the organisation you work within changes, sometimes you change, sometimes both. Consider this a normal state of affairs.

It is always acceptable to backtrack from a previous position. However, it is not, of course, acceptable to claim that you never had the opinion you expressed before. You need to be able to explain what has changed, and why. Sometimes you even need to admit you were plain wrong. This strengthens the authority of anyone in a leadership position.

If you don't think that such backtracking can strengthen your own position, you probably didn't have any real authority in the first place. But it can still be built. The cases where it truly is too late are rare. Start by building trust.

In Touch with Your Inner Sheepdog

As if herding two-legged cats isn't complicated enough in itself, the one herding those cats is, in fact, also a cat. Being a cat myself, I really should understand how impossible this task is. I won't even attempt to answer the question of why I still took on the challenge, except by saying that the only viable answer lies in the question. It's difficult, and therefore, it is fun.

This is the scenario. As a leader of cats, I must be the cat who acts as a sheepdog. Barking instead of meowing. But barking is not enough.

As a leader, you are not just part of the gang. Understanding this is fundamental to doing a good job. The boss is not on an equal footing with the subordinates. As the volunteer chairman of an association, you find yourself in a sort of middle ground. Even there, you are no longer just part of the group, but someone expected to maintain your official persona.

Suddenly, people whom I was only superficially acquainted with came to me with their concerns. Suddenly, I was expected not to have an opinion in general but to explain the association's position. I was, indeed, one of the members, but I was also the one expected to take responsibility, and, above all, be the one who gets everything that goes wrong on their plate. In this situation, it's crucial to not try to act like just any cat going about its business, but also to be in true contact with your inner sheepdog.

So, what does a sheepdog really do? It keeps track of the herd by circling around it. It makes sure the herd stays together, and while not everyone will move together, the herd as such will move on in a common direction. Plus, the sheepdog occasionally barks. There might even be an occasional, literal "woof." I have applied this tactic in committee meetings, with good results. People laugh a bit, and they understand what it means. But, of course, it's essential not to overdo it. It's not just a joke.

The essence here is to step into the role. It's not me personally speaking; it's the chair. But sometimes, of course, it's very much me. This is the difficult part. The sheepdog should be available, but the best sheepdog is always the one who can lead the herd without barking much. Otherwise, there is the risk that barking becomes nothing more than a boring background noise.

An important part is to create routines based on the rules specific to the case. However, not everything can be regulated in detail. It is essential to be able to act in a spirit that aligns with the rules without the rules themselves needing to be expanded into absurdity.

Then there will always be objections. The larger the number of smart people assembled, the more objections. There will be occasions when those presenting the objections are perfectly right. Fortunately, I am confident enough to be able to say, "Yes, those were good arguments. I retract my previous position and assert the opposite." Sometimes, however it's crucial to recognize the moment when it's time to say, "I've heard your arguments, but we're still doing it this way."

You need to be able to bring out the authority that the sheepdog needs but also to show that deep down, it's still a cat herding the cats. It's always allowed not to agree, but once a decision is reached everyone must comply with it.

So, it's essential to have a good connection with your inner sheepdog. It's also crucial to step into the role with the right measure of moderation. This is something we all learn by doing, step by step in different positions.

Very Stupid and Quite Exhausted
Memoirs of a Swedish Mensa dinosaur, VI

At the General Meeting, during the Annual Gathering 2017, I was re-elected chair, for a second two-year term. The very same evening, we had the by now traditional big semi-formal dinner, followed by the main party of the gathering. I did not stay particularly late, as I had to chair the first board meeting with the partly new board the next morning. But some people party all night on these occasions. And out of the approximately 400 members taking part that year, unfortunately there were around 20 who misbehaved badly that night. Some of them climbed onto the hotel roof – luckily no one fell down from it. Some were shouting and, worse, drinking in the corridors outside their rooms. (Bringing your own drink anywhere other than to your room is strictly prohibited in Swedish hotels.) When hotel staff asked them to stop, the response was such that the staff called the Police for help.

Next morning, I woke up to the tale of several problems during the night. As chair, it was now my responsibility to handle. I had a talk with the ombudsman, of course, and we agreed on how to proceed regarding him trying to find out who did what and whether to recommend any specific measures within the organisation. Then, I went to the hotel reception, apologized profusely for the members in question, ensured that the manager as well as the staff knew that Mensa Sweden and its chairperson certainly did not condone such behaviour. I simply did my best to minimize damage.

And then, I did something truly stupid. As rumours were running high, I posted a short text to the members only Facebook group for the meeting. There, I reported about the problem – not naming anyone, of course – and stated that I was ashamed of the small group of members behaving this way. I added that I had thought of using some Haddockisms, but that this small group did not deserve such niceties and could only be called "bloody idiots". All this to a members only group ... Within 20 minutes, the text was published on the website of the local newspaper. Why it was considered interesting enough to make it into national news I will never quite understand, and certainly not how it spread to news in several other countries. But believing that something posted to a members only group with several hundreds of

Mensans would stay part of internal communications, was probably the most publicly stupid thing I have ever done.

The waves did settle after a few weeks, with normal board work and normal association everyday problems back in the foreground of my Mensa time. National work, international work, all the everyday things. I was getting tired, though. The next year, after the 2018 Annual Gathering and General Meeting, I felt that I was counting down to the day I would leave all the everyday grind to the next chair.

At the 2019 General Meeting, Mensa Sweden decided to be part of creating the Nordic Mensa Fund. That is a legacy I am very proud of, and it would also be part of my continued Mensa-related volunteer work. Of course, the boards I led got many things done, while the membership of Mensa Sweden continued growing, from around 5000 to 7000 in the four years I chaired the association. But the Fund is a major legacy.

Closing the chapter of being chair felt wonderful. I knew that the organization would be in good hands with the next chair, and that my part was done. Those years as chair had been interesting and rewarding but also exhausting. It was the kind of experience I was happy to have had but would never want to repeat.

Enter the Role Without Being an Actor

There are many situations where, in the eyes of others, you are in your role. Not acting as a professional actor does but being in the role for the moment. This chapter is about stepping into the role. We all do sometimes, subconsciously. Knowing how and when to decide to do so helps in many leadership tasks.

Role Depending on Context

Most of us show certain sides of ourselves at work, while other aspects, which are evident with close friends or family, remain excluded. Typically, this doesn't mean that we're pretending to be someone else at work, but that we only reveal certain things. We choose, more or less consciously, to show parts of a complex personality. Similarly, in larger groups, most of us show only certain sides. If you belong to several such groups, you usually show slightly different facets of yourself in each. Perhaps the persona you display at a sports club is somewhat different from the one you show at a parent-teacher meeting – not radically different, but with certain aspects either exposed or highlighted to different degrees.

Just as someone stepping into a leadership position at a company is expected to slightly change what they present in that role compared to being part of a team at work, so is a person assuming a position of trust in an association expected to at least partially step into a new role. What that role looks like depend on the position. The role of chair is primarily a leadership position, but so are some others. They are similar to leadership positions in the corporate world, except that in a non-profit organisation, they rarely come with payment or a clear right to choose one's colleagues.

The Role of the Chair

There you are, about to step into the role. Time to bring out the qualities that will enable you to function as chair. Patience will be needed; probably more patience than you might think possible. You'll also need something that allows you not to take the inevitable criticism directed at the chair too personally. A generally thick skin is an advantage, but most importantly, you must be able to distinguish between the role and the person, even when it's your own. "They're talking about the chair, not about me specifically," is a highly useful strategy, or at least it has been for me.

In your role, you need to find a role persona that still feels genuine, both outwardly and inwardly. Additionally, you must bring forth your ability to listen to expressed suggestions as well as to more inarticulate needs. The part of your personality you use to decide what should and should not be passed on from a conversation is also essential. This is a skill most adults possess and rarely reflect on as long as it works, but it is an important one.

To complicate matters further, the role of chairperson looks slightly different in the various contexts you will encounter within the framework of the role. When dealing with the board, the qualities that help drive decisions while also ensuring that everyone has a proper say are clearly needed. I was aware from the start that I needed to balance my "commanding" tendencies with bringing along everything I had in terms of curiosity about other people, humour, and understanding.

When dealing with officers appointed by the board, the role is more akin to that of a manager. However, you must always remember that these people are doing things for the organisation because they want to, that they are not being paid for their work, and that it is important to ensure they continue to want to do the work. Not an easy task, but part of the role.

In relation to members at large, the chair has a representative role. Here, it's important to look for the aspects of yourself that feel appropriate to showcase but also align with what a sufficient number of members want to see. This is not always easy, and it can be particularly difficult to balance what you show to your friends within the organisation with what you present as chair to everyone. Remember there will be situations when your friends also need to hear the chair speaking, rather than you as a private person.

Then, there will also be the role of being a public face for your organisation. In the public role, you are indeed entirely public. It is certainly easier to temporarily adopt a more pronounced mask, if necessary, but of course, you ideally want to avoid having to do so.

Keep your Distance to the Role

One of the most beautiful compliments I have ever received came from a Mensa member who, after we had to navigate a particularly difficult annual meeting, said she was proud that the organisation had a chairperson who would firmly withstand a storm. Internally, I didn't feel particularly firm, but it was a moment when I had brought forth the calm and composure I could muster. When I heard her assessment, I felt that I had succeeded in my role.

Regardless of whether the leadership role is part of your day job or a volunteer position, let it remain a role. Let your more private reactions and feelings hide behind it. The role is a projection, half a step in front of you. To be able to use it, you need to be aware that it is separate from you, keep this separation, and bring forth the aspects of yourself that you believe correspond best to that role.

Brains Just Want to Have Fun

When I give talks about my experiences leading intelligent people, I sometimes start by asking if anyone in the room has never been bored. So far, no one has raised their hand in response to that question. The day it happens; I will seriously consider whether I will dare repeat it at the end of the lecture...

Being bored at times is perfectly normal, but no one wants to be bored for long. The brain wants to have fun, and that means it needs something to think about. This applies to everyone, of course. However, the highly intelligent often seem more prone to boredom, which intuitively seems logical. A brain with greater capacity to think needs more stimulation to feel it is working properly. This does not necessarily mean needing more to do; rather, it means needing more variety so that what one does provides some intellectual stimulation.

Stress from lack of stimulation

The most dangerous stress is indeed the kind that leads many to burnout: not knowing what is expected, receiving contradictory directives, and never being able to feel satisfied that a task is completed. But one should not underestimate the stress that arises when the brain is under stimulated.

This is highly relevant in the workplace. You can get stressed from having so much to do that you can never keep up, but you also get stressed from not having enough to do. It seems that a brain that gets nothing to work on eventually becomes overloaded from sheer boredom.

On the long run, having but a little to do is generally very stressful. This is especially true in workplaces where employees cannot use excess work time to read books, watch films, or take a language course to keep their brain busy when work tasks run out. If you are a bit lucky, you might find your stimulation outside the workplace, for example in voluntary work for an association, but the best is naturally to create a situation where the brain can have fun in multiple contexts, ideally including not being directly bored during working hours.

While volunteer work in itself usually doesn't require that you spend time just waiting around for the working day to finish, it also needs variation in order not to be boring. Thus, it's important to let volunteers ease into new tasks when they start getting bored.

The Pippi Longstocking Principle

An intelligent person with healthy self-confidence is often able to live by the quote from children's book character Pippi Longstocking: "I've never tried that before, so I'm sure I can do it!"

Admittedly, you need to be aware that it usually takes some time to master new tasks. But that is part of the point of learning new things. The brain has fun when it gets to try something new. This can and should be utilized, in good workplaces but also very much so in an association like Mensa. Allowing volunteers to try something completely new is part of a continuous building up and rebuilding, to keep the society healthy.

This is also a reason not to expect volunteers to stay in the same role for very long. Once you know an area and have had time to accomplish what you wanted there, it starts to get boring. As a leader, observing that point is an excellent opportunity to suggest to someone who is starting to get bored that they take on some other tasks instead. One advantage of having Mensa members to lead is that volunteers are often willing to try new roles and do new things. This is what our brains enjoy.

Leadership is Lonely

To be the leader of a group, regardless of the type of group, is a lonely task. This is a fact known to every manager who takes their work seriously, as well as anyone who has taken on the role of leading an association. Being a leader not only includes responsibilities, but also the obligation to keep certain matters to yourself. Many of those are, of course, shared within a small group, such as the board of a volunteer-based organisation. However, just as there are things a company leader cannot share with their staff, there are also things a Mensa chairperson cannot share. This is part of the position, and anyone taking it on must be prepared to handle a certain loneliness.

Knowing That You Cannot Share Everything

First and foremost, anyone in such a position must understand that, regardless of how it feels, the position will inevitably be perceived as one of power. With power comes responsibility. We all know this. And with power comes a certain degree of distance. Of course, fellow members of an association remain, first and foremost, comrades. Naturally, any board that functions even remotely well consists of people willing to share responsibilities and do their part. That said, there will be situations where the chairperson cannot share certain matters even with the rest of the board.

You can, of course, discuss your association-related concerns with a close friend outside the organisation. Similarly, a company leader might talk about work problems with a friend outside the industry. These friends can listen and offer sympathy, which is undoubtedly valuable. But they do not know the organisation and, therefore, can rarely provide real advice.

Find Your Peers

One of the many purposes of the annual Mensa International Board of Directors meeting, aside from the formal decisions made there, is to allow the chairs of the various national Mensa associations to meet and converse outside the meeting room. It is, as one colleague put it during such an occasion, a relief to hear that others encounter the same crazy troubles as you do. Naturally, many good ideas and inspiring successes are also shared, but perhaps the most important aspect is the opportunity to discuss problems with others who understand how the organisation works, and who have or have had similar challenges.

At least to me, it was even more important to have the same kind of exchange at a regional level. The occasions when the chairs of the four Nordic associations meet provide an excellent safety valve, an opportunity to talk about everything that isn't quite working out; everything that, by necessity, weighs on the chairperson's shoulders. This in itself brings relief. Also, four heads can usually come up with more ideas than one. You can gain new perspectives, suggestions, and advice on what has or hasn't worked in neighbouring countries. A key prerequisite for these meetings is that everything said remains confidential, and that even before we get to know each other, everyone knows from the start that, on this level, we can trust one another.

If I were to offer one piece of final advice, it would be to seek out others in equivalent positions and make a point of sharing experiences, but above all, to provide each other with this safety valve. Finding your peers and ensuring that you can talk openly is essential. The fact that you may also make friends in the process is a pleasant side effect.

To Be Continued

I have continued to volunteer in Mensa after my two terms as chair of Mensa Sweden. International volunteer work, that had already been there for years, came into focus.

In fact, the international volunteering had also been part of my Mensa experience since the 1990s. I have mentioned it only briefly in this book, but it grew in importance to me after my chairing years. There are stories to tell of encounters, fun and challenges in that work too. And of course, I have continued to learn about leadership, from gains and from mistakes. There will be a second part to this tale.

Mensa Links

To read more about Mensa, and find out how to join if you are not already a member, start at the Mensa International page

mensa.org

Each national Mensa also has its own website. The one I'm a member of, Mensa Sweden, is found here

mensa.se

I also recommend a look at the site of the Nordic Mensa Fund, to read about how the Fund supports intelligence research and how you can support the Fund.

nordicmensafund.org

Thank You

To everyone who commented on "Konsten att valla katter", or on any of my talks on the topic of herding cats, thank you for providing input and ideas.

To all the Mensans I have met, been led by or tried to lead, thank you for the experience and may it always continue.

A special thank you to the patient test readers, who helped me shape this English version. Galit, Martyn, Melanie, Erik, Palo: again, thank you!

Any remaining errors or Swedishisms are entirely my own.

Stockholm April 2025

Monika Orski